SOWING AND GROWING

THE PARABLE OF THE SOWER AND THE SOILS

By Marilyn Lashbrook

Illustrated by Stephanie McFetridge Britt

ME TOO!
B O O K S

Treasure!

Fort Collins, CO
800-284-0158

"Sowing and Growing" will help you prepare the soil of your child's heart to accept and obey God's Word. Children are fascinated by gardening, and though young children will not follow the symbolism, this story is a good springboard to teach the importance of really hearing and learning God's Word.

Pause to allow your child to follow the directions on pages 20 - 29. Praise your child for the positive ways in which he responds to God's Word. Encourage him to do better in one area. If your child is not memorizing Scripture on a regular basis, this would be a good place to start. Preschoolers have an incredible ability to memorize, once they understand the concept. A child of 3 - 5 can easily memorize a substantial verse each week if you repeat it with him once or twice a day.

Preparation of the soil is the first step to having a fruitful garden. Carefully and lovingly prepare the soil of your child's heart to receive the Word of God. Water with tears and prayers. Scripture says you will doubtless reap with rejoicing. (Ps 126:6)

Library of Congress Catalog Card Number: 93-086767
ISBN 0-86606-450-8

Art direction and design by
Chris Schechner Graphic Design

SOWING AND GROWING

THE PARABLE OF THE SOWER AND THE SOILS

By Marilyn Lashbrook

Illustrated by Stephanie McFetridge Britt

Taken from Matthew 13, Mark 4 and Luke 8

ME TOO!
B O O K S

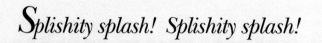

Splishity splash! Splishity splash!

Jesus sat in a little boat. People stood on the
shore. Jesus told them a story
– a story about something they saw every day
– a story about a farmer planting his field.

There once was a farmer who went out
to scatter seed on his field.

Where did the seed land?
  Some fell on the road,
– some on the rocks,
– some among thorns.
But most of the seed fell on the good, soft soil.

Pickety peck! Pickety peck!

Hungry birds ate the seeds on the road.

Poppity pop! Poppity pop!

The seeds on the rocks popped up in a hurry!
But the soil was so thin, the little seedlings
shriveled and died.

Scritchity scratch! Scritchity scratch!

The thorn bushes scratched and choked the
little sprouts growing among them.

But the seed that fell on the soft, damp soil
sprouted and grew.
Some seeds grew a little.
Some grew more.
Some grew a lot of wheat.
The farmer was pleased with his crop.

After Jesus told the story,
his friends wondered about it.

"What does the story mean?," they asked.
So Jesus answered their question.

"The story is like a picture . . . a picture to make people think about themselves."

Jesus explained that there are different kinds of soil. And there are different kinds of people.

Some people have a chance to hear Bible
teaching. But they do not really
   look . . .
      or listen . . .
         or think about
what the teacher says. And because they do
not listen, they never learn about God's love.

*Point to the part of your body you use to listen to
God's Word.*

*Point to the part of your body you use to look at your
parents and teachers when they speak to you.*

*Point to the part of your body you use to think about
what the Bible teaches you.*

Some people hear about Jesus and believe in Him. But they do not learn Bible verses to help them grow.

When trouble comes, they choose to do the wrong things. Soon they forget they ever knew Jesus.

Point to the part of your body you use to learn Bible verses word for word.

Point to the part of your body you use to say "NO!" when someone tries to get you to do bad things.

Some people hear God's Word and believe.
But they care more about other things.
Instead of growing and sharing, they think
only of themselves.

*Point to the part of your body you use to come when
your parents call.*

Point to the part of your body you use to give to others.

Some people love God.
They love God's Word, the Bible.

They grow and grow and grow
as they learn and obey God's Word.

They pray and sing to the Lord. They help others learn about Jesus.

Point to the part of your body you use to sing and pray and speak for God.

Point to the part of your body you use to be helpful to others.

Point to the part of your body you use to walk to meet new friends at school and church.

Some people tell a few friends about Jesus.
Some tell more people about Jesus.
And some tell many others about Him.

Jesus is very happy with people who
　　listen . . .
　　　　　and believe . . .
　　　　　　　　and grow . . .
　　　　　　　　　　　and share.

Books for Ages 2-5

SOMEONE TO LOVE
The Story of Creation

TWO BY TWO
The Story of Noah's Faith

I DON'T WANT TO
The Story of Jonah

I MAY BE LITTLE
The Story of David's Growth

I'LL PRAY ANYWAY
The Story of Daniel

WHO NEEDS A BOAT?
The Story of Moses

GET LOST, LITTLE BROTHER
The Story of Joseph

THE WALL THAT DID NOT FALL
The Story of Rahab's Faith

NO TREE FOR CHRISTMAS
The Story of Jesus' Birth

NOW I SEE
The Story of the Man Born Blind

DON'T ROCK THE BOAT!
The Story of the Miraculous Catch

OUT ON A LIMB
The Story of Zacchaeus

SOWING AND GROWING
The Parable of the Sower and the Soils

DON'T STOP . . . FILL EVERY POT
The Story of the Widow's Oil

GOOD, BETTER, BEST
The Story of Mary and Martha

GOD'S HAPPY HELPERS
The Story of Tabitha and Friends

Readers for Ages 5-8

IT'S NOT MY FAULT
Man's Big Mistake

GOD, PLEASE SEND FIRE!
Elijah and the Prophets of Baal

TOO BAD, AHAB!
Naboth's Vineyard

THE WEAK STRONGMAN
Samson

NOTHING TO FEAR
Jesus Walks on Water

THE BEST DAY EVER
The Story of Jesus

THE GREAT SHAKE-UP
Miracles in Philippi

TWO LADS AND A DAD
The Prodigal Son

NOBODY KNEW BUT GOD
Miriam and Baby Moses

MORE THAN BEAUTIFUL
The Story of Esther

FAITH TO WIN
The Story of Caleb

BIG ENEMY, BIGGER GOD
The Story of Gideon

Available at your local bookstore or from

Treasure Publishing

Fort Collins, Colorado
1-800-284-0158